ABOUT
MAMMALS

PUBLISHER	Joseph R. DeVarennes	
PUBLICATION DIRECTOR	Kenneth H. Pearson	
ADVISORS	Roger Aubin	
	Robert Furlonger	
EDITORIAL SUPERVISOR	Jocelyn Smyth	
PRODUCTION MANAGER	Ernest Homewood	
PRODUCTION ASSISTANTS	Martine Gingras	Kathy Kishimoto
	Catherine Gordon	Peter Thomlison
CONTRIBUTORS	Alison Dickie	Nancy Prasad
	Bill Ivy	Lois Rock
	Jacqueline Kendel	Merebeth Switzer
	Anne Langdon	Dave Taylor
	Sheila Macdonald	Alison Tharen
	Susan Marshall	Donna Thomson
	Pamela Martin	Pam Young
	Colin McCance	
SENIOR EDITOR	Robin Rivers	
EDITORS	Brian Cross	Ann Martin
	Anne Louise Mahoney	Mayta Tannenbaum
PUBLICATION ADMINISTRATOR	Anna Good	
ART AND DESIGN	Richard Comely	Ronald Migliore
	George Elliott	Sue Wilkinson
	Greg Elliott	

Canadian Cataloguing in Publication Data

Main entry under title:

Questions kids ask about mammals

(Questions kids ask ; 14)
ISBN 0-7172-2553-4

1. Mammals—Miscellanea—Juvenile literature.
2. Children's questions and answers.
I. Smyth, Jocelyn.   II. Comely, Richard.   III. Series.

QL706.2.Q47 1988   j599   C89-093084-8

Questions Kids Ask . . . about MAMMALS

continued

What is a mammal?

What do bats, monkeys, whales, kangaroos and giant armadillos have in common? They're all mammals—and so are you.

Mammals are air-breathing animals with backbones. They are warm-blooded, which means they can maintain a constant body temperature regardless of the temperature around them. They are born alive and as babies take milk from their mother's body. And finally, mammals all have hair—at least for a while. (In case you're wondering, whales are born with hairy whiskers, but in most cases the whiskers soon fall off.)

Mammals are found everywhere from the Arctic ice cap through the tropics to the edge of the Antarctic. They live in deserts, jungles, mountains and in the water. Some even fly through the air.

Mammals vary in size from the shrew, which weighs 2 grams (.07 ounces) and is 80 millimetres (3 inches) long, to the blue whale, which weighs 107 metric tons (214,000 pounds) and is 33 metres (108 feet) long.

What do bats eat?

If you were to invite a bat for dinner what would you serve? In most cases, insects would be just the thing. But some kinds of bats prefer a larger diet. The flying fox bats in Africa and Asia, for instance, eat only fruit. The noctilio bats of South America eat fish. Hummingbird bats mostly eat pollen and flower nectar. The large spear-nosed bats of tropical America will eat almost anything from bananas to hamburger to smaller bats!

The famous vampire bats of South and Central America have inspired horror stories for hundreds of years. The truth is that they do bite animals and drink their blood—so do mosquitoes after all—but they don't drain away all of the blood.

In fact, about 15 millilitres (one tablespoon) is a full-course meal for a vampire bat!

Vampire bats rarely bite humans and the idea that you will become a vampire if you're bitten by one is only a myth.

DID YOU KNOW . . . bats that looked very much like the ones we see today were flying on the earth more than 50 000 000 years ago!

6

Are bats blind?

You have probably heard the expression "as blind as a bat," so you may be surprised to learn that bats are not blind at all. In fact, some species see quite well. However, since bats fly at night most of them rely on their ears rather than their eyes to find their way around.

In order to catch insects and avoid obstacles, bats use a system known as *echolocation*. As they fly, they emit as many as 200 high-pitched sounds a second. These sound waves bounce off objects and back to the bats' oversized ears. By analyzing the echoes the bat can not only tell how far away an object is but what it is. A bat can track down and capture a flying insect in less than one second!

DID YOU KNOW . . . echolocation, or sonar, is a method used by ships and boats to navigate.

Do bears sleep through the winter?

Have you ever heard someone say they "slept like a bear"? They are usually talking about a long, deep sleep where nothing disturbed them. Some bears do sleep for a long time. When winter comes, black bears that live in cold, northern climates snuggle down into a slumber that may last as long as six months. They are not alone. Their cousins the grizzlies also take long winter naps.

Some people call this hibernation but it is actually a "winter sleep." Hibernation means that the heart rate and breathing slow down and the animals enter a state where they can't be woken up until their own body clock tells them it's the right time. Only a few animals, like frogs and ground squirrels, do this. Bears simply sleep deeply and wake up during warm spells to roam around outside, taking a look at what winter has to offer.

Can all monkeys hang by their tails?

Wouldn't it be fun to swing by your tail from a tree? You may think that all monkeys can do this. But it isn't true.

Only New World monkeys, that is those found in Mexico and Central and South America,— and not even all of them—have tails that can hold onto things. Those that do have these special gripping, or *prehensile,* tails can use them to support their entire body weight, leaving their hands *and* their feet free to gather food.

Old World monkeys live in Africa and Asia. They may have a short tail, a long tail or even no tail at all! But they never have a gripping *prehensile* tail and therefore cannot swing by their tails.

Why don't gorillas climb trees?

A fully grown gorilla would rather not. The heavier a gorilla becomes, the more difficult it is for it to climb. Adult gorillas *can* climb trees, but they find it easier to move their heavy bodies along the ground. Young gorillas are much smaller and lighter. They spend a lot of their time climbing and playing among the upper branches of trees.

Which ape is the best acrobat?

By far the most graceful and acrobatic ape is the gibbon. It never seems to stop moving. It is a small, slender-bodied animal, weighing less than 8 kilograms (17 pounds). It has extremely long hands and lightweight bones that help it to swing easily through the highest tree tops. Gibbons move so rapidly at times that they appear to be flying. They can leap as far as 15 metres (50 feet) in a downward direction. And they are so well co-ordinated they can even catch a flying bird.

Gibbons are found in Southeast Asia and the East Indies. They have very thick fur and come in a variety of colors, from buff to black. Some species even change color during their lifetime. They feed mainly on fruit, leaves and buds and also enjoy insects, birds and eggs.

Why do whales "sing"?

Recently scientists studying humpback whales were surprised to discover that these giant mammals could make beautiful, haunting sounds. While most whales make a variety of sounds, humpback whales are the most vocal. Researchers found that the whales sing different songs at different times. These songs are the loudest and longest calls in nature. Some last 30 minutes.

Scientists are not sure why whales sing. Perhaps some songs are simply greeting calls, a way of keeping in touch with other whales of their kind as they move through the vast depths of the ocean. Some songs may be a way to tell other whales where there is food. Since the songs change with the seasons, some may be "love songs" to let other whales know where they are during the mating season.

Why do whales spout?

Like all mammals, whales need air, and they breathe it through an opening, or blowhole, on the top of their head. It is closed tightly when they are under water but when they surface to breathe they open it with a great "whoosh" and force the used air out of their lungs. When you see this it looks like a spout of water but it's actually water vapor. Just as you can see your breath on a cold day, the whale's warm breath

Can dolphins talk?

Dophins are such playful animals we often wish they could talk to us. The sounds you make when you are talking are produced by your vocal chords. But dolphins could never make human sounds because they don't have any vocal chords.

Nevertheless, dolphins do spend a lot of time talking to each other. Scientists believe that a dolphin can make as many as 2000 different sounds by blowing different amounts of air through its blowhole.

Dolphins use their language of whistles, squeaks, creaks, chirps and clicks to keep in touch with the other members of their group. If a dolphin swims into danger, it will alert its friends.

You may have heard a dolphin in a marineland making squealing sounds when jumping out of of the water. This is not real dolphin language. It is a sound that the dolphin has been taught by its trainer.

can be seen when it hits the colder ocean air.

You can even tell whales apart by the shape of their spout—the gray whale's is short and bushy, the blue whale's is tall and skinny and the right whale's is shaped like a heart.

DID YOU KNOW . . . sperm whales can dive 3 kilometres (2 miles) below the ocean's surface and hold their breath for nearly two hours.

Can dogs climb trees?

How come we always hear stories about cats getting stranded in trees or up telephone poles but we never hear the same stories about dogs? Are dogs simply smarter or do they know how to get down?

Neither, as a matter of fact. Dogs don't get stranded up trees or poles for the simple reason that they don't climb them in the first place.

Dogs are built to run swiftly and their feet and claws are designed to propel their bodies over the ground. Dogs' claws are also often used for rapid digging, and unlike cats' claws, they cannot be drawn into the paw.

Cats have flexible paws with a strong grip, and their claws are hooked to dig into things. As a result, a dog simply hasn't got the right equipment to climb —something most cats find out very early in life!

I can wait.

Why do dogs turn around before lying down?

Dogs were once as wild as their wolf relatives, and they still have many instincts of their wild ancestors. One of these is to turn around before lying down. Wild dogs had to make their beds in grass or drifted leaves. By walking around in a circle, they trampled a flat place for a bed. They also left a wall of standing grass around their bed to hide them from enemies.

Even though your pet dog isn't in danger of being attacked and has a nice, warm rug to curl up on, the instinct to circle around on its bed before lying down is still there.

Why do dogs bury bones?

Have you ever gone grocery shopping with your parents? They usually buy food to eat over the next few days or weeks or sometimes even longer. Animals stock up on groceries too. Squirrels bury nuts, and some meat eaters, such as wolves, bury leftover food in the ground or hide it in a hollow log. Because dogs are close cousins of wolves, they too will bury a favorite food, like a bone, so they can come back to it later.

Wow! That was a big job.

Do opossums "play possum"?

Has anybody ever said to you "Oh, you're just playing possum"? What they mean is that you are just pretending to be asleep or hurt or whatever. This saying comes from a trick that the opossum, or possum, actually plays. And this trick can be a matter of life and death!

Many animals consider the opossum a tasty meal. Unfortunately opossums aren't designed to protect themselves and they are clumsy runners. When danger threatens they take refuge up a tree. But what if the nearest tree is too far away? Opossums have developed a trick to deal with that situation too. Its enemies won't eat a dead animal, so when they approach, the opossum drops dead. Well, not

really, but it puts on a very good act. It flops down on its side with its tongue lolling out of its mouth. It slows its heart rate and breathing and may close its eyes. The pursuer can nudge it, pick it up and even shake it with no response. Eventually the attacker will leave and the opossum is safe to "return to life."

I'm pretty sure it's going to rain today.

Can a porcupine shoot its quills?

Porcupine quills are sharp, painful and hard to remove, but they are a great way for porcupines to protect themselves. Imagine how amazing it would be if porcupines could actually shoot their quills as many people say they do. Well, fortunately for innocent passersby, the porcupine must wait for an intruder to come close enough to touch. The quills are attached loosely to its body and tail and break off on contact with the intruder's skin. Many curious dogs have come too close and run off yelping, their face full of quills. Sometimes quills do fly out when a porcupine moves quickly but these fly helter-skelter and land wherever gravity takes them.

Can groundhogs predict the weather?

"Yes, folks, here we are again. It's February 2, National Groundhog Day, and we are waiting patiently for the groundhog to predict when spring will be here."

It's an old superstition, brought to North America by the British and the Germans. People used to believe that if the sun was shining on February 2 and the groundhog saw its shadow, it would be frightened and would return to its underground home for the remaining six weeks of winter. But if the day was cloudy, the groundhog wouldn't see its shadow, would stay above ground and spring would come early. However, scientists have not proved that the groundhog is a reliable weather forecaster.

DID YOU KNOW . . . in Europe it is bears and badgers that are supposed to forecast the arrival of spring.

How do beavers build dams?

Imagine the life of a beaver: gnawing at trees until they fall, dragging them great distances, then working underwater to build a dam of mud and sticks. What is the beaver's reason for doing this?

Beavers build their homes in ponds, and these must be deep enough not to freeze all the way through in winter. The entrances to a beaver lodge are underwater, and the beaver family must be able to get in and out to find food even when the top of the pond is frozen. By building a dam across a stream, the beaver eventually blocks the outflow of water. Like a giant plug the dam holds the water in and a deep pond is created, making it the perfect place for beavers to live.

What do beavers use their tails for?

Everyone recognizes the beaver by its broad, flat tail that looks like a squashed pine cone. You would think that a tail that looks this unusual must have some special uses—and it does.

The beaver uses its tail both on land and in the water. On land, when a beaver stands on its hind legs to chop down a tasty tree, its tail helps it to keep its balance. Underwater, the tail becomes a rudder to steer the beaver as it swims. It also works as a balance when the beaver is towing a heavy log. And the sound of a beaver slapping its tail on the water as it dives warns other beavers of possible danger, and they dive too.

As you can see, the peculiar-looking tail comes in handy.

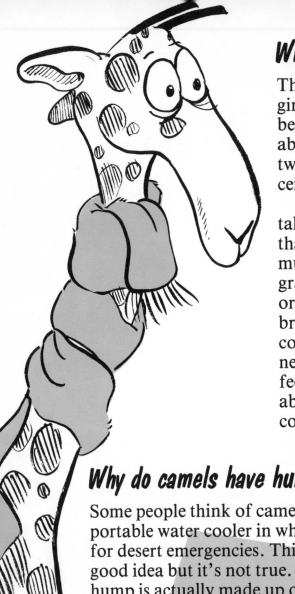

Why are giraffes so tall?

The tallest living animal is the giraffe. A bull giraffe's head may be as high as 5.5 metres (18 feet) above the ground. That's over twice the height of an average ceiling in a house.

Giraffes were not always so tall. Scientists know from fossils that prehistoric giraffes were not much taller than a horse. Giraffes gradually grew longer necks in order to reach food that other browsers (woody stem eaters) couldn't reach. With their long necks, giraffes are now able to feed on the top of trees, well above the reach of their nearest competitors.

Why do camels have humps?

Some people think of camels' humps as a sort of large portable water cooler in which the camels carry water for desert emergencies. This would seem like a good idea but it's not true. The camel's hump is actually made up of fat. Camels live in very harsh climates where food is often scarce, and for long periods they may have to rely on this stored fat for the energy they need to survive.

There is another benefit to having humps. They

Are horns the same as antlers?

Moose have antlers, goats have horns, but what about yaks?

Many animals have horns or antlers growing out of their heads. Horns and antlers look quite a bit alike. They come in pairs and they are found on top of the head near the ears.

Antlers are found on members of the deer family. They are a special type of fast-growing bone located on top of small bumps on the animal's skull. Except in the case of caribou and reindeer, antlers are found only on the males. Typically they begin to grow in the spring, and by the fall, the males look impressive and are ready to do battle for the perfect mate. The antlers then fall off, only to grow again next year.

True horns are found on members of the sheep, goat, antelope and cow families— and that includes yaks. They are found on both males and females. Horns are joined directly to the skull. They begin to grow when the animals are young and, except for an accident, they remain in place and continue growing all the animal's life. Horns are made up of a bony core covered by hardened protein for protection.

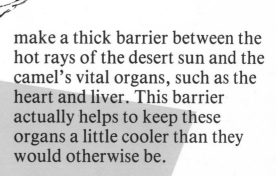

make a thick barrier between the hot rays of the desert sun and the camel's vital organs, such as the heart and liver. This barrier actually helps to keep these organs a little cooler than they would otherwise be.

Do house mice live only in houses?

When you watch cartoons or read fairytales, you begin to think that mice live only in people's houses and that they spend their lives tormenting cats with many narrow escapes.

Mice certainly do live in people's houses—houses are dry, warm, relatively safe, and usually there is some form of food around. But mice are wild creatures and live not only in houses but in just about every place you can imagine. There are mice in the Arctic, in the deserts and high up in the mountains. They are found nesting in almost every marsh, forest, field and grassland in the world. Since they are so small, they can make their homes in any tiny nook or cranny. They live in burrows, tree stumps, under masses of grass and even in snow houses. And when they live near humans, people have found mice nesting in old shoes, car engines and inside old tin cans. To a mouse, any place can be home!

Do mice like cheese?

Mice live almost anywhere and eat almost anything, including cheese. Their reputation for loving cheese probably dates back to the early days of their association with people.

A long time ago, when there were no refrigerators or freezers, only some foods could be stored. Cheese kept well and it was stored wrapped in cloth or sealed in wax. Mice are always quick to find a free meal and the smell of cheese is stronger than that of many foods. A quick chew and there was dinner. Since people often found mice nibbling their stores of cheese they thought that this was a mouse's favorite food instead of just the easiest one to find!

Are elephants really afraid of mice?

Have you ever seen a cartoon that shows a huge elephant running in fear from a tiny mouse? The belief that elephants are afraid of mice has been around for a long time, but it is simply not true.

Zoo directors and circus trainers agree that elephants pay no attention to the mice that run through their barns. Someone even went so far as to try an experiment: mice were tossed to an elephant in a zoo, and the elephant simply sniffed at them and turned back to its peanuts.

If elephants aren't afraid of mice, what are they afraid of? Well, it depends on how many elephants you're talking about. A lone elephant will show a fear of dogs and human beings. But a herd of wild elephants isn't afraid of a thing. If provoked, they've been known to attack people, cars and even houses! Who would be silly enough to provoke a herd of wild elephants?

Why does a kangaroo have a pouch?

Newborn human babies can look awfully small and helpless. But they look like giants compared to a newborn kangaroo. A brand new kangaroo, or joey, is about the size of a jelly bean! It is blind and deaf and so under-developed that eyes, ears and back legs haven't even appeared. The joey uses its strong front legs and powerful sense of smell to make its way into its mother's pouch. Though the distance is not very far, the joey is so tiny and helpless that it would be the same as you climbing a ten-storey building just using your arms!

Once inside the pouch, the baby kangaroo attaches onto one of its mother's nipples. For several months it will stay safe and warm inside, drinking milk and growing larger and furrier and ready to face the world outside its mother's pouch.

What animal has a bill and webbed feet like a duck, lays eggs like a chicken and nurses its young like a cow?

Give up? It's the duckbilled platypus, an amazing animal.

Because it nurses its young with milk as mammals do, the platypus is a true mammal.

But most mammals have noses and lips. The platypus has a leathery bill, which it uses to poke worms, insects and small animals out of river banks. It has no teeth but uses the hard ridges on its bill to grind food.

All four of its feet are webbed, which makes it an expert swimmer. Its toes end in sharp claws, which it uses to dig tunnels in stream banks where it builds a nest.

In the nest the female lays from one to three eggs. When the eggs hatch, the mother uses her tail to hold the naked young platypuses close to her body to nurse.

How high can a kangaroo jump?

The kangaroo is nature's champion high jumper. With a push from its long, powerful hind legs, a kangaroo can jump as high as 2 metres (6 feet).

Kangaroos can cover 8 metres (26 feet) in a single leap. When the pressure is on, a kangaroo can make these enormous jumps while traveling at speeds of up to 65 kilometres (40 miles) per hour.

The front legs of a kangaroo are very small and not nearly as strong as the hind legs. They are only useful when the kangaroo crawls on all fours, which it usually does when it is looking for food.

The kangaroo's long, thick tail is very important for helping it balance while hopping. When it's not moving it stands upright, the tail and hind legs acting as a tripod. This position enables the kangaroo to use its eyes, nose and ears to detect enemies. If an enemy comes along —BOING—the kangaroo bounds away, leaving it far behind.

DID YOU KNOW . . . male platypuses have spurs on their hind legs connected to poison glands in their body. In a fight, they will dig their claws into the enemy and release the poison.

Since platypuses won't live in zoos, you can only see them in Australia.

What color are rhinoceroses?

There are two kinds of rhinoceroses that live in the southern half of Africa, the Black rhinos and the White rhinos. But neither kind is black or white—they're both a muddy gray. Why? *Wyte* was the name given by early Dutch-speaking settlers to one group of rhinos that had a wide (*wyte* in Dutch) upper lip. Later settlers who spoke English misunderstood and thought that *wyte* meant "white." And if one rhino was white, the other must be black.

There are other rhinos too—the Asian rhinoceros that lives in India, and a dwarf species that lives in Indonesia. They're both colored muddy gray too.

Why do zebras have stripes?

A zebra's stripes run all over its body and usually on its ears, mane and tail too. No two zebras look the same; each one has a different pattern of stripes, just as humans all have different patterns of fingerprints.

The zebras' stripes help to hide them from their enemies. They

live in grasslands, and their stripes look like grass being blown in the wind when they are walking. When they lie down, they are almost totally hidden as their stripes blend in with the long grass.

But if the stripes are supposed to look like grass, why aren't they green? You must keep in mind that most animals are color-blind. The zebra is and so is its main enemy, the lion, who sees everything as black and white—even green grass!

Why do hippopotamuses carry birds on their backs?

Have you ever seen the comic with the chatting bird perched on the back of a hippo? This is not as fanciful as it might seem.

Certain types of birds, like egrets and oxpeckers, do stand on all sorts of large animals including hippos, oxen and rhinos. The bodies of the giant hosts are crawling with ticks and other insects. The birds perch there for an easy-to-reach snack. Along with their meal, they get a free ride and are safely out of the reach of predators.

And what does the large host get out of it? Well, a good clean-up of the annoying pests it can't reach itself and an extra lookout for danger. It's a pretty good deal for everyone concerned.

Why does an elephant have a trunk?

One of the most amazing natural "animal tools" is the elephant's trunk. It has thousands of muscles and it can daintily pluck a blade of grass or, with incredible power, lift an entire tree! The trunk is made up of parts that are found in the nose and upper lip of other animals. These parts are joined into a long sensitive tube. At its tip there are one or two "fingers," depending on the type of elephant. These fingers have many nerve endings so that the elephant can feel what it touches. The inside of the trunk is just like the lining of your nose, and the elephant has an excellent sense of smell.

Some people think that elephants drink through their trunk but if you have ever gotten water up your nose when you've been swimming you'll know how awful it feels. The elephant sucks water up into its trunk, up to 5 litres (20 cups) with each snoutful, and then sprays it into its mouth for swallowing—leaving its nose free to breathe!

DID YOU KNOW . . . an elephant keeps cool by using its ears! The ear of an elephant is as big around as a wheelbarrow and probably weighs twice as much as you do! Each ear is lined with a network of blood vessels. When the elephant feels hot, it waves its ears back and forth like a fan. This flapping cools down the blood in its ears and when this blood travels through the elephant's body it cools off the entire animal.

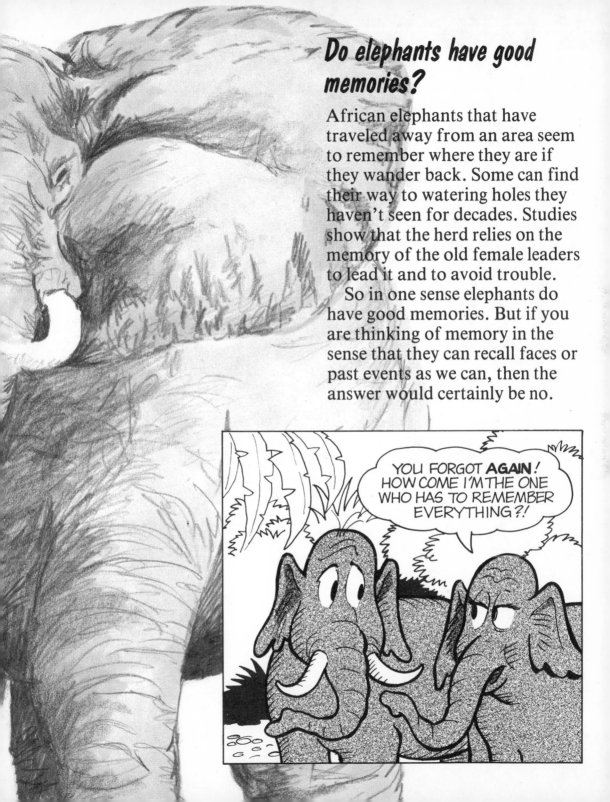

Do elephants have good memories?

African elephants that have traveled away from an area seem to remember where they are if they wander back. Some can find their way to watering holes they haven't seen for decades. Studies show that the herd relies on the memory of the old female leaders to lead it and to avoid trouble.

So in one sense elephants do have good memories. But if you are thinking of memory in the sense that they can recall faces or past events as we can, then the answer would certainly be no.

Are sloths lazy?

Sloths move in slow motion all the time. But the fact that sloths never hurry doesn't mean that they are lazy.

Sloths only eat leaves and leaves don't provide a lot of energy. Being slow actually helps the sloth to survive. Everything about sloths is designed to save energy. They have extra long necks that enable them to reach leaves without moving their bodies. They even grow green algae on their fur so that they can hide from enemies among the green tree leaves and don't have to run away from danger. Sloths are not lazy. They are just good energy savers.

What is the fastest land animal?

A yellow body covered with black spots is prowling silently through the tall grass. Seeing an antelope grazing nearby, it crouches low, and then it charges. The antelope gallops away, but in seconds it is pinned to the ground.

The cheetah is the only meat-eating mammal that can overtake an antelope. Over short distances, it is the fastest animal on earth.

From a resting position cheetahs can reach a speed of 72 kilometres (45 miles) in 2 seconds! In full stride, they can run as fast as 113 kilometres (70 miles) per hour. That's faster than most cars travel on the highway!

How fast can horses run?

Different kinds of horses can run, or gallop, at different speeds. Work horses have been bred to be large and heavy for pulling heavy loads, so they do not run very quickly. Riding horses are lighter. Any good riding horse can gallop at about 50 kilometres (30 miles) per hour for short distances.

Of course, race horses can gallop the fastest. The Quarter Horse has been bred especially for running races that are only 400 metres (a quarter of a mile) long. (Other race horses run races that are longer than this.)

The world record for speed is held by a Quarter Horse, Big Racket, who ran 400 metres (a quarter of a mile) in 20.8 seconds in 1945. Big Racket was running 69 kilometres (43 miles) per hour. In 1973, a horse named Secretariat ran a race of almost 2 kilometres (1-1/8 miles) at a speed of over 61 kilometres (38 miles) per hour, also a world record.

Do raccoons really wash their food?

When we prepare food for dinner we do all sorts of things to it. We cook most of it and before that we peel, wash, chop, slice and grind. Compared to most other creatures in the animal kingdom, we are pretty picky about our food.

Take raccoons for instance. People often say that they wash their food to make sure it's clean. But would an animal that eats frogs, fish and crawdads whole be bothered by a few specks of dirt? Not really. Raccoons enjoy playing with their food before eating it, however, and since they feed near water, they often play with it *in* the water. That is probably how these stories originated—though a raccoon may dip an occasional frog or toad into the water to wash away the bitter coating that sometimes covers it.

Do lemmings really jump into the ocean?

For centuries, stories have been told of strange happenings in Norway—thousands of small brown and white lemmings suddenly leaping off seaside cliffs. Some people thought that this was a case of mass suicide, but study has led to a more reasonable explanation.

Like many small mammals, lemmings have lots of babies when their supply of food is plentiful. And with only two months between each litter, it doesn't take long for the lemming population to get out of control. Suddenly there are no places left to live, food is scarce and the lemmings are forced to migrate. Norway is a mountainous country with all sorts of ocean inlets, and some lemmings are bound to

What is a gnu?

The gnu (sounds like "new") is the native name for one of the many kinds of antelope that roam the plains of Africa.

The gnu is certainly a mixed-up looking animal. It has a slender, long-legged body like a horse; short, heavy horns like an ox; a massive head and shoulders, and a mane and beard like a bison. It runs with long, stiff-legged strides, hardly seeming to touch the ground, and can travel all day at this trot.

When in danger, two of the biggest males put on a mock battle, hoping to scare their enemy away. They lower their heads and kick each other furiously as if to prove how wild and fierce they are. No wonder their other name is *wildebeest*.

DID YOU KNOW . . . there are over 3500 species of mammals in the world today.

come across these in their travels. They are moving so quickly that they plunge headfirst off the cliffs, driven on by the lemmings behind them!

Index _____